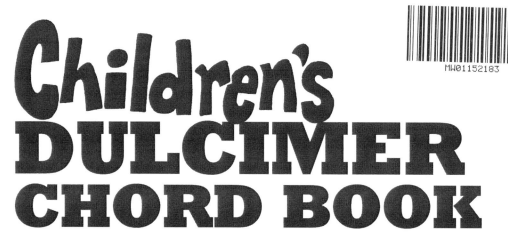

Children's DULCIMER CHORD BOOK

by Lee "Drew" Andrews

MW01152183

Table of Contents

Cover Instrument: Folkcraft Teardrop Mountain Dulcimer FCT1 Model. Courtesy of Folkcraft Instruments. www.folkcraft.com

Special thanks to Richard Ash at Folkcraft Instruments, Inc.

This book is written for instruments with a 6 1/2 fret.

2 3 4 5 6 7 8 9 0

Visit us on the Web at www.melbay.com — E-mail us at email@melbay.com

How to Read Chord Diagrams

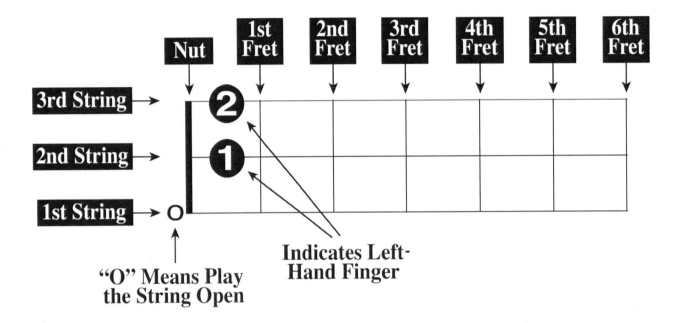

- Vertical lines are frets
- Horizontal lines are strings
- Circled numbers are left-hand fingers
- Small "o" over a string means to play the string open (no fingers pressing down)

The chord fingerings in this book are not set in stone.
If there is a fingering that works better for you then please use it.

DAD

D Chord

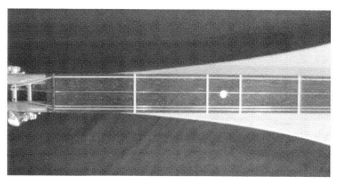
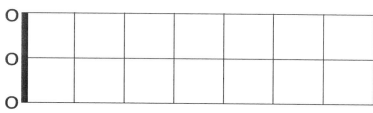

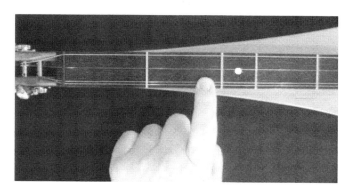
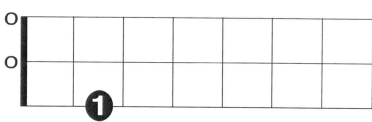

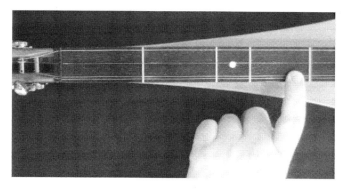
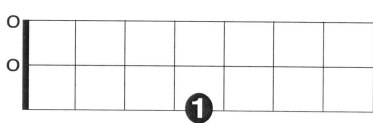

Play

D

DAD   G Chord

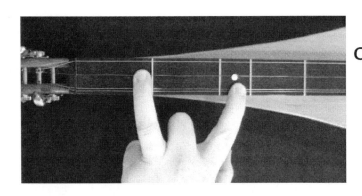
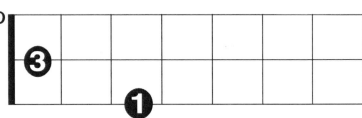

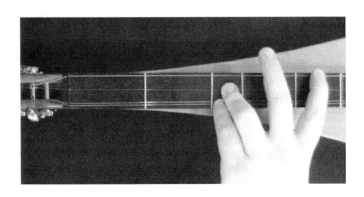
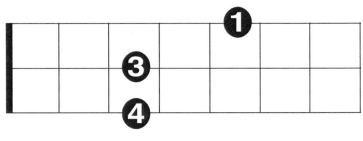

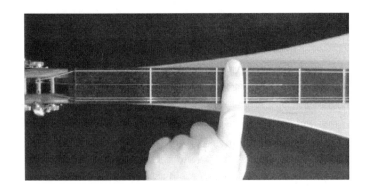
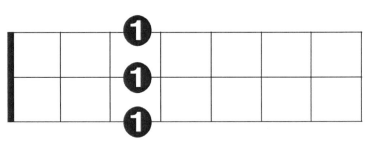

Play

D   G   D

| / / / / | / / / / | / / / / ||

DAD   A Chord

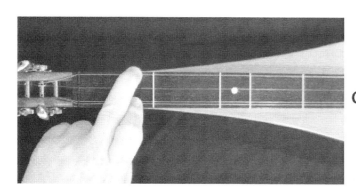
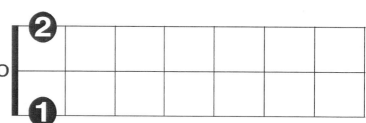

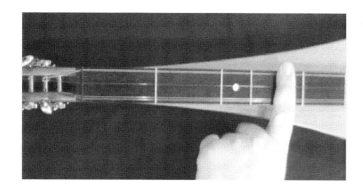
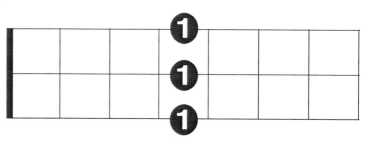

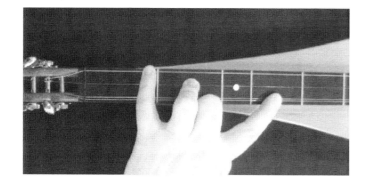
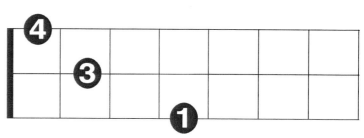

Play

D	G	A	D
/ / / /	/ / / /	/ / / /	/ / / /

DAD   A7 Chord

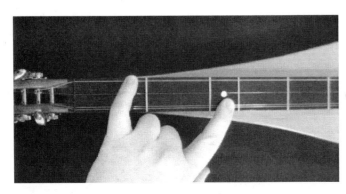
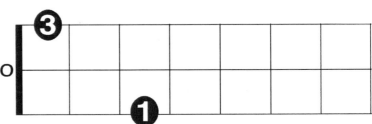

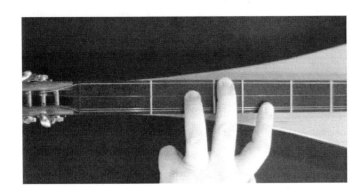
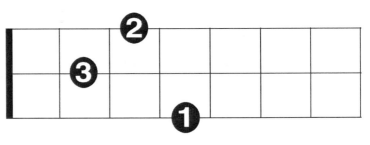

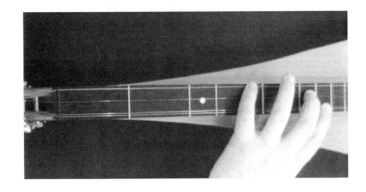
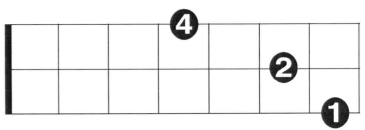

DAD   Em Chord

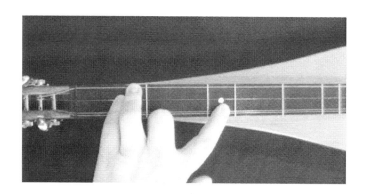 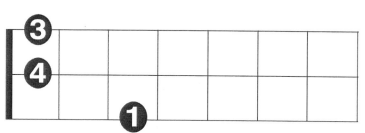

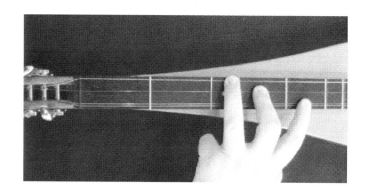 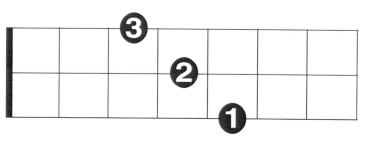

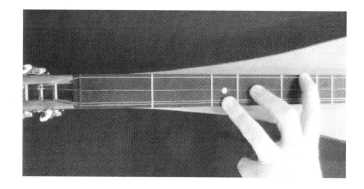 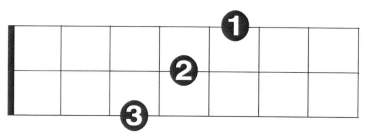

| Play |

D   G   Em   A7   D

| / / / / | / / / / | / / / / | / / / / | / / / / ‖

DAD   Bm Chord

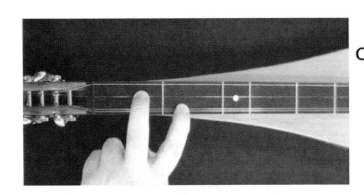
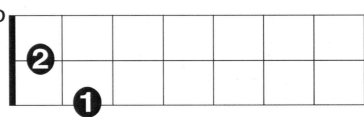

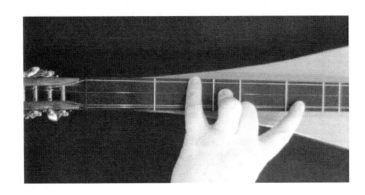
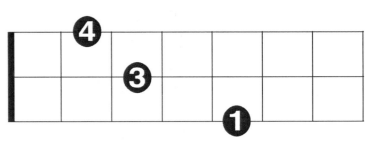

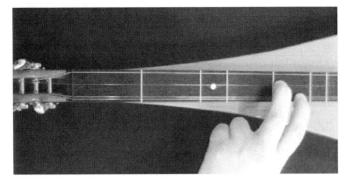
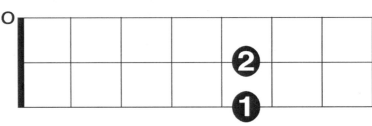

Play

D	G	Bm	Em	A7	D

| / / / / | / / / / | / / / / | / / / / | / / / / | / / / / ‖ |

DAD　　　　　F#m Chord

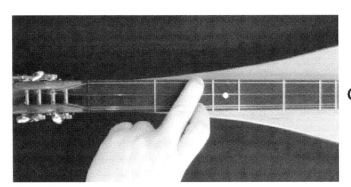 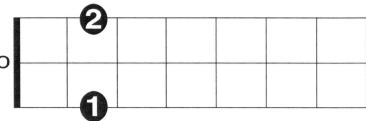

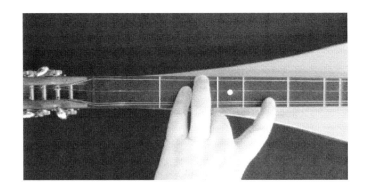 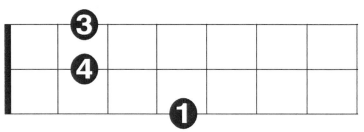

Play

| D | G | F#m | Bm | Em | A7 | D |

| / / / / | / / / / | / / / / | / / / / | / / / / | / / / / | / / / / | / / / /‖

DAD

C Chord

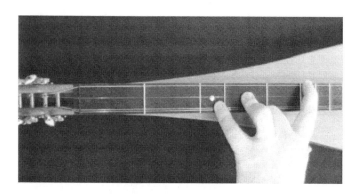

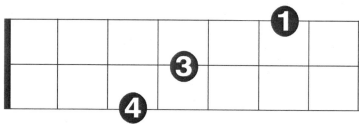

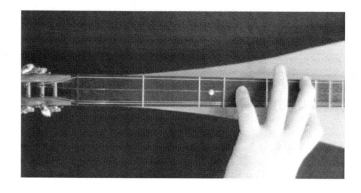

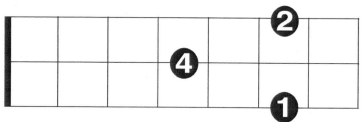

Play

| C | Em | C | G | C |

| / / / / | / / / / | / / / / | / / / / | / / / / ||

DAD   F♯ Chord

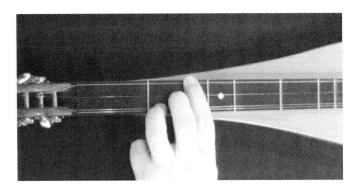
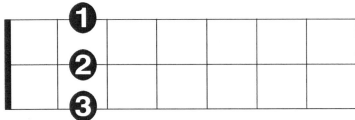

Play

| D | Em | F♯ | F♯m | G | A7 | D |

| / / / / | / / / / | / / / / | / / / / | / / / / | / / / / | / / / / ||

DAD   G△7 Chord (G major 7)

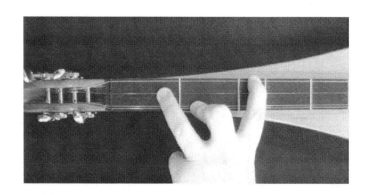

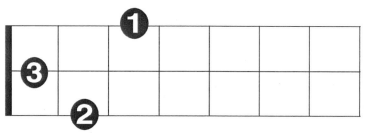

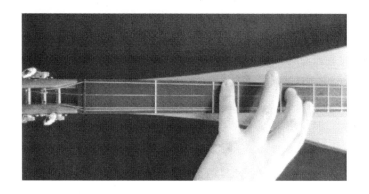

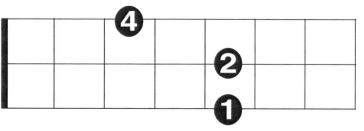

Play

D	G△7	A7	D
/ / / /	/ / / /	/ / / /	/ / / /

DAD   Em7 Chord

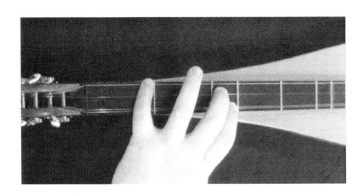
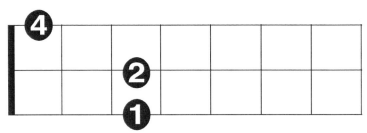

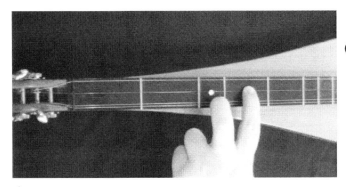
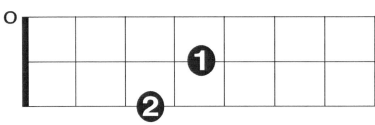

Play

D   Bm   Em7   A7   D

| / / / / | / / / / | / / / / | / / / / | / / / / ‖

DAD   Am Chord

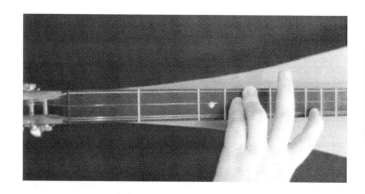
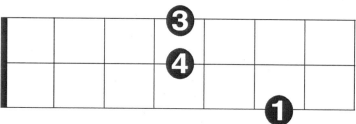

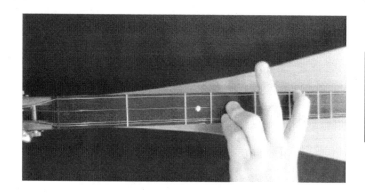
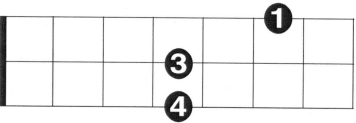

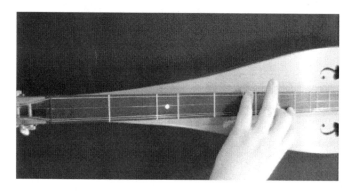
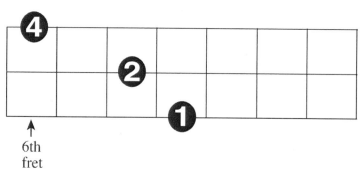

6th
fret

Play

G△7	Em	Am	D	G
/ / / /	/ / / /	/ / / /	/ / / /	/ / / /

14

DAD　　　　E Chord

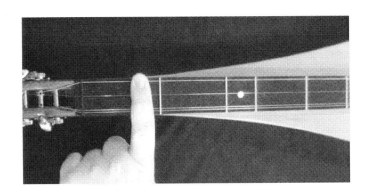 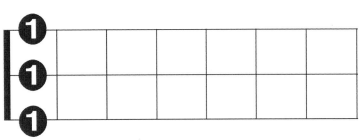

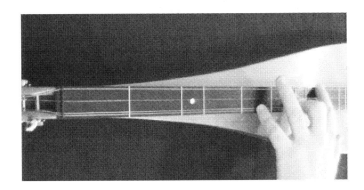 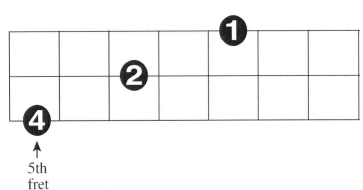

5th
fret

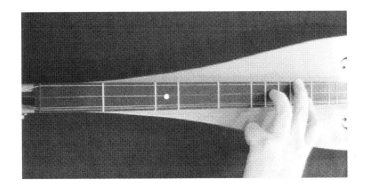 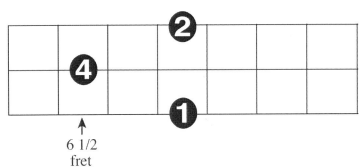

6 1/2
fret

Play

A	F#m	Bm	E	A
/ / / /	/ / / /	/ / / /	/ / / /	/ / / /

F#m	Bm	E	A
/ / / /	/ / / /	/ / / /	/ / / /

15

DAD   E7-Em6-Em9 Chords

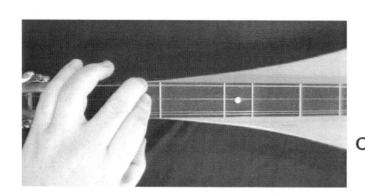

E7 (or Em7)

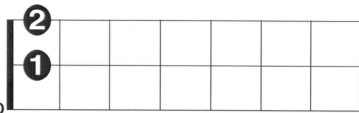

Em6 (or Edim)

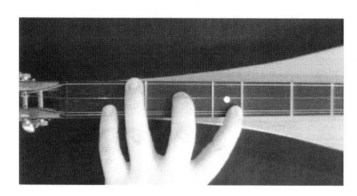

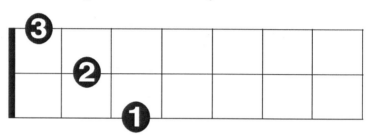

Em9

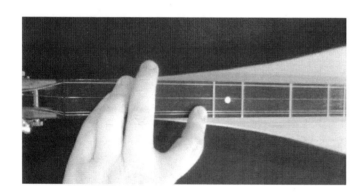

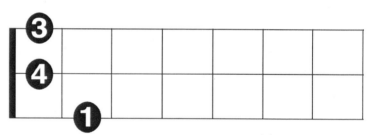

Play

A	D	Bm	E7	A
/ / / /	/ / / /	/ / / /	/ / / /	/ / / /